The Library of Explorers and Exploration

SIR FRANCIS DRAKE

Circumnavigator of the Globe and Privateer for Queen Elizabeth

Joy Paige

the rosen publishing group's

rosen central

To Brooke a[...]*ery special sisters*

Published in 2003 by The Rosen Publishing Group, Inc.
29 East 21st Street, New York, NY 10010

Copyright © 2003 by The Rosen Publishing Group, Inc.

First Edition

Library of Congress Cataloging-in-Publication Data

Paige, Joy.
Sir Francis Drake : circumnavigator of the globe and privateer for Queen Elizabeth / by Joy Paige. — 1st ed.
    p. cm. — (The library of explorers and exploration)
Summary: A biography of British pirate and explorer Sir Francis Drake, featuring his search for riches in the Americas and his eventual voyage around the world.
Includes bibliographical references and index.
ISBN 0-8239-3630-9 (library binding)
1. Drake, Francis, Sir, 1540?–1596. 2. Great Britain—History, Naval—Tudors, 1485–1603—Biography. 3. Great Britain—History—Elizabeth, 1558–1603—Biography. 4. Explorers—Great Britain—Biography. 5. Privateering—History—16th century.
6. Admirals—Great Britain—Biography. 7. Voyages around the world.
[1. Drake, Francis, Sir, 1540?–1596. 2. Great Britain—History, Naval—Tudors, 1485–1603. 3. Great Britain—History—Elizabeth, 1558–1603. 4. Explorers. 5. Admirals. 6. Voyages around the world.]
I. Title. II. Series.
DA86.22.D7 P35 2003
942.05'5'092—dc21

                                                              2002000481

Manufactured in the United States of America

CONTENTS

Introduction: Master Thief of the
   Unknown World   5
1. Drake's Early Life   11
2. Exploring the New World   20
3. Drake the Commander   31
4. The Famous Voyage   43
5. Finding Riches   56
6. Wealth and Fame   66
7. Later Voyages   75
8. The Legacy of Sir Francis Drake   87
Chronology   100
Glossary   102
For More Information   104
For Further Reading   106
Bibliography   107
Index   108

Habes Lector candide fortiss. ac invictiss. Ducis Draeck ad vivum Imaginem qui tota terrarum orbe, duorum annorum, et mensium decem spatio, Zephiris suetis tibi circumducto, Angliam sedes proprias. 4. Cal. Octobr. anno á partu Virginis 1580 reuisit cûm antea portu soluisset id. Decem: anni 1577.

INTRODUCTION

MASTER THIEF OF THE UNKNOWN WORLD

S ir Francis Drake's life was nothing short of exciting and full of adventure. His humble beginnings fueled his desire for riches, fame, and respect, all of which he achieved before his death in 1596. He became one of the richest men in England and was well known throughout his native land. In fact, he was the most famous man in England for 200 years. Drake's work made England a country to be reckoned with.

Before Drake's birth, Ferdinand Magellan had begun a journey around the world but had died before the trip was completed. Another man from Magellan's expedition, Juan Sebastian Elcano, is credited as the first to complete a journey around

Sir Francis Drake, navigator and privateer, is one of the great explorers of English history. Drake and his crew were the first Englishmen to circumnavigate the globe, claiming a part of California for England along the way. He was celebrated for fighting the invasion of the Spanish Armada in 1588 but was also hated by the nobility for his humble origins.

the world. Drake was the second explorer, and the first Englishman, to successfully complete a journey around the globe. While sailing, Drake made numerous geographical discoveries, helping to clear up confusion about the location of certain lands and adding to what was already known about lands in the New World and beyond.

Drake was a pirate, a person who acquired wealth by stealing it from other people. The main goal of most of Drake's voyages was to steal valuable goods, especially gold, from Spain, or to force the people living on Spanish settlements to give him money or goods. Drake's hatred of Spain and King Philip II started in 1568, when Spanish vessels attacked English sailors on a voyage and took many men captive. He sought revenge for many years, using his dislike for King Philip to fuel his passion for piracy.

Queen Elizabeth I was in power during the time that Drake made his fortune, and it was their close relationship that helped Drake along the path to success. Spain and England had been bitter enemies for many years, and Spain was much more powerful than England. Rather than accept this and allow Spain to grow even more powerful, Queen Elizabeth secretly allowed Drake to journey to Spanish towns in the New World and wreak havoc on their settlements. It was a great honor for Drake to be able to have the queen as a friend, and their relationship was strong. She did not allow others to sway her opinion of him, and he in turn put her on a pedestal, brought her extravagant gifts from his voyages, and even named an island he discovered after her.

But Drake's life was not without failure. His power and wealth made him an easy target for criticism from other influential people in England. Some believed that his background made him undeserving of the fame he received. Others believed his ego drove him to mishandle matters with Spain. But through it all, Drake stuck to his beliefs and did not let others get in the way of his goals. Drake was headstrong and powerful. He knew what he wanted and went to any means to get it.

Drake lived in a time when disease and lack of scientific study made untimely deaths quite common. On his voyages, many of the crew perished because of disease that could be cured. Scurvy was a common illness that sailors suffered on long journeys. We now know that scurvy is a result of a deficiency in vitamin C, but back then, no one knew the cure. It was common for members of Drake's crew to be crippled by illnesses that we now know are easily cured.

The long voyages that Drake took were physically and mentally challenging. Imagine being confined on a ship for months, without even seeing land. As captain on many of

In 1579, Christopher Saxton published his *Atlas of England and Wales*, the first complete collection of county maps of the kingdom and one of the first national atlases ever produced. He made a general map and thirty-four county maps that were printed separately from 1574 to 1578 and issued together as an atlas in 1579. They are considered landmarks of British mapmaking and printing.

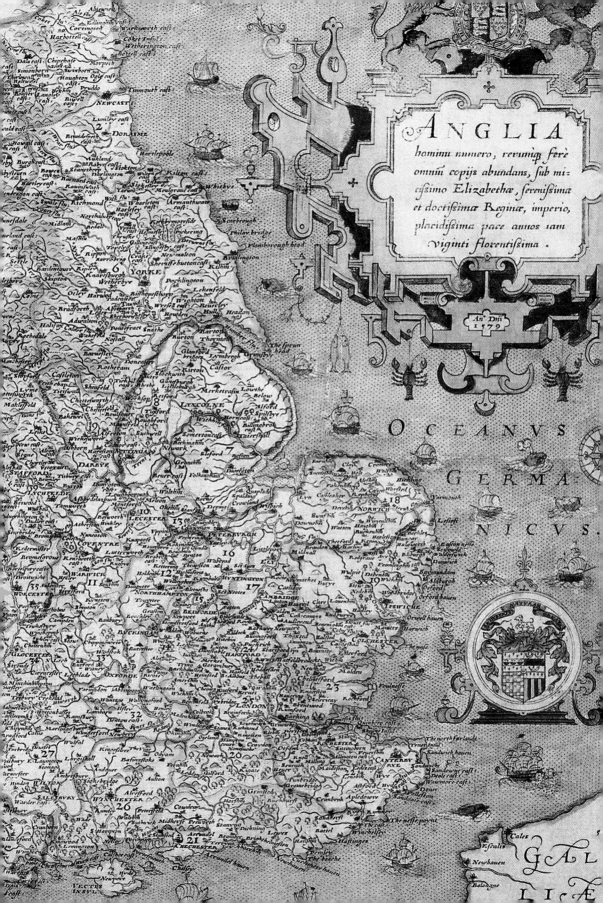

his voyages, Drake was responsible for his crew. If they ran out of food and fresh water, which happened on occasion, he was to blame. It was also commonplace for fighting to occur between his crew and others. Some of the sailors were killed or taken captive during these battles. Drake's job had the potential to earn him great fame and honor, but it was also extremely demanding.

It's no wonder that Drake became the most famous man in England, both hated and loved by so many. His discoveries were impressive, and his voyages resulted in gold, silver, jewels, and other items of worth for England. He was dubbed the master thief of the unknown world, a title that suited him well.

1

DRAKE'S EARLY LIFE

He was more skilful in all points of navigation than any . . .
He was also of perfect memory, great observation, eloquent
by nature.

—John Stow on Sir Francis Drake

Francis Drake's life has been documented in books, periodicals, and historical documents for hundreds of years, but most of the information is conflicting or lacking in detail. The details of his later life are hard to understand because he, his family, and the English government purposely embellished and obscured the truth about Drake and his voyages. To make matters more confusing, there is not much information on Francis Drake's early life. But it seems this is the way Drake wanted it; he even told lies and covered up the truth about himself. What we do know about Drake's early life helps us to understand how he was prepared for a life at sea.

The Drake Family

Francis Drake was born on the Crowndale farm on land owned by Tavistock Abbey in Devonshire in southwestern England. The exact date of his birth is unknown, but the best estimate is February or March 1540. At the time of Francis Drake's birth, there was a lot of social change in England, and Tavistock was changing dramatically.

Francis's father, Edmund Drake, was a skilled craftsman. He was one of the few who knew a certain technique to soften cloth. His job was not enough to support his family, however, so he sought out another occupation: He became a Protestant preacher. But because this part of England was still largely Catholic at that time, the Drakes were discriminated against for their Protestant beliefs.

There is not much information available about Francis's mother or siblings. It is believed that Edmund married a woman named Anna Myllwaye, and that together they had twelve children, Francis being the oldest. But even that is unclear. It has been documented that the twelve children may have been a combination of siblings and cousins.

Drake's family was fortunate for the time: His father leased a large amount of land and was able to support the family through farming. English farmers usually worked the fields with large plows and rotated the crops they planted.

The Drake family came from a long line of farmers. They held the lease on a great deal of land, and they earned their living farming that land. After Henry VIII took lands from Tavistock Abbey in 1539, the family struggled. Though their lease was renewed in 1546, religious disturbances and uprisings in 1548 drove the Drakes to Kent, where Edmund Drake took work as a preacher. Young Francis was sent away to help lessen the load.

Francis Drake's First Voyages

When Francis Drake was about thirteen years old, his family sent him out to sea. Young Francis worked full-time on a small cargo ship owned by

Edmund Drake: Criminal?

Edmund Drake's financial difficulties apparently lead him to a brief stint as a criminal! On December 21, 1548, he was convicted along with others for stealing a horse and assaulting a man on two separate occasions for which he was later pardoned. It is rumored that this was, in part, why the Drake family left Tavistock.

Many young men were sent to sea by their parents to learn the sailing trade. Francis Drake went at thirteen when the Drakes fell into poverty.

an older man. The owner taught Drake how to sail and provided him with food and shelter. Among other things, the young sailor learned how to read a compass and handle the boat in different kinds of weather. This knowledge would prove invaluable in later years. In fact, these beginning voyages were the foundation of Drake's career.

Drake became very close with the ship's master, who had taken a liking to the young man. He made life on the boat pleasant for Drake, even though apprentices on ships were accustomed to harsh conditions and poor treatment from the ships' masters. Drake, it seemed, had lucked out. The master of the voyage treated him like a son. After the owner died in 1560, he left the ship to Drake. After a few years as the master of the ship, Drake sold it in order to seek adventure. He wanted a more exciting life for himself. He ended up in Plymouth.

Sixteenth-century navigators relied upon compasses such as this one to find their way across the great oceans.

Life in Plymouth

A number of Drake's relatives were living with the Hawkins family in Plymouth. The Hawkins family was related to the Drake family, and it was not uncommon during that time for people to send their children to live with relatives. In Plymouth, Drake was formally educated. He learned about trade and politics. He was exposed to a more educated and sophisticated set of people than those he had known in Tavistock. Plymouth was very different from the farming community that Drake grew up in. In Plymouth, Drake's ideals began to form,

The city of Plymouth, England, is a vital port and naval base. On July 24, 1440, it became the first borough in England to be created by an act of Parliament. In 1588, the fleet defending England from the Spanish Armada met at Plymouth. It was from Plymouth that Sir Francis Drake, Sir Richard Hawkins, Sir Walter Raleigh, and several other explorers set forth on their expeditions. It was the last port touched by the *Mayflower* on its voyage to America.

English admiral Sir John Hawkins led extremely profitable expeditions in 1562 and 1564. He captured slaves on the West African coast, shipped them across the Atlantic Ocean, and, despite Spanish prohibition, sold them in Spanish ports in the West Indies. Drake joined him on his ill-fated voyage of 1566.

and he started to see a broader version of the world than he was used to.

It was not unusual for members of the Hawkins household to go on sailing voyages and to steal from other ships. The act of stealing valuable goods from ships is called piracy. Pirates were the people who carried out these crimes. At the time, piracy was an offense that usually went unpunished. Drake would later make a name for himself by stealing from other vessels.

In 1566, a Hawkins family ship was sailing to the New World, and Drake was appointed second in command. The captain, John Hawkins (1532–1595), taught him about navigation, or the steering and directing of the ship. He also learned what sea fighting was like, something that he would become accustomed to in later years. On this voyage, his ship attacked a Portuguese ship that was carrying valuable goods. They took slaves, ivory, wax, and sugar from the Portuguese vessel.

But this voyage was not a complete success. Hawkins's sailors attempted to force Spaniards to trade goods for the slaves the Englishmen had taken from the Portuguese. It was customary for the English to sell the slaves they had acquired, and they weren't used to the opposition they now faced. Hawkins and his men went back to England without anything to show for themselves. The voyage was not a success, but it was an important experience for Francis Drake.

2

EXPLORING THE NEW WORLD

Drake had suffered much in person and property from the Spaniards, and had vowed vengeance and retribution. His friends fitted out five vessels for him to go on a voyage of discovery and plunder.

—Excerpt from Volume 1 of *Our Country*,
published in the late 1800s

Although Drake's first trip to the New World was not a success, he was nevertheless asked to be an officer on John Hawkins's next voyage to the New World. In September 1567, John Hawkins was preparing a fleet of ships to sail to the Caribbean, and it was an honor for Drake to be hired. John Hawkins wanted Drake on the same ship he would be sailing on, the *Jesus of Lubeck*.

During the sixteenth century, English warships underwent design changes that would have a major impact on the history of the world. Responding to pressures from the major European land powers, English monarchs were forced to realize that, as an island nation, England's best defense lay in a strong navy. English shipwrights experimented with various designs that would enable them to keep their country from being invaded.

Their journey began with a fleet of six ships, some of them specially built for combat. Warships, as they were called, carried cannons on board. The men were especially prepared for combat, not wanting this trip to be their last. They were determined to return from this voyage with valuable goods.

The Start of the Voyage

The Englishmen began their journey by raiding Portuguese settlements around the African coast and in the Cape Verde Islands. This raid was quite successful, since they not only took slaves but also acquired more ships to take with them as they sailed to the New World. The three ships they stole were used to hold the extra cargo they had picked up. But since they suddenly had extra vessels, they had to appoint men to work on them. Drake was put in command of one of the ships, the *Gracia Dei*, the "Grace of God."

He was later put in command of the *Judith*, a fifty-ton ship. Along with a number of other ships that also held slaves, Drake and his men sailed along to the Caribbean to sell the 400 slaves they had stolen. They reached their destination in March 1568.

In the New World, they expected to sell their slaves at a hefty price. But, once again, they hadn't anticipated the opposition they would face. The Spaniards were under

This image shows slaves prospecting for gold. The Europeans made huge profits from the slave trade, which expanded and enriched their economies. Forced labor, brutal suppression, and exposure to European diseases devastated the enslaved populations.

orders to refuse all offers to purchase slaves from Englishmen. At the first port, the colonial governor merely turned down the Englishmen's offer. However, things weren't so civil at the next stop.

Opposition

Hawkins and his men were cautious at the next port they stopped in, Rio de la Hacha. Only two of their ships were sent ahead, and the rest stayed behind and waited. The two ships that went ahead, the *Judith* and the *Angel*, ran into trouble. Not only did the Spanish refuse to buy slaves, but they also shot at the English seamen. To retaliate, the Englishmen directed a cannonball at the home of the town's governor, Miguel de Castellanos.

A few days later, the rest of the fleet arrived. John Hawkins tried to appeal to de Castellanos by requesting permission to sell their slaves, but the governor would not budge. He didn't want to lift the ban on buying slaves from English sailors. Hawkins decided to retaliate.

Armed with weapons, 200 Englishmen left their boats for the shore. They captured Rio de la Hacha and forced the government to buy about 200 of the slaves they had on board their ships. But they weren't satisfied; they were merciless in their revenge. Not only did they demand that the slaves be purchased, they also forced de Castellanos to pay a ransom to keep the seamen from destroying the town.

Robbery on the high seas was a lucrative, though dangerous, vocation. Originally, pirates were ordinary criminals, but with the development of rich sea trading routes, governments sponsored piracy.

At the next port, Santa Marta, in modern-day Colombia, the men found that the Spaniards living there were easy to do business with. They were in desperate need of slaves, and they didn't mind breaking the law put in place to ban Spaniards from buying slaves from Englishmen. Approximately 110 slaves were sold to the residents of Santa Marta, and the sailors went on their way to other Spanish towns.

Unfortunately for the Englishmen, the people in the other towns they stopped in did not want to purchase the slaves they had. But instead of persisting, they

This 1560 chart of what is now Morocco shows the Canary Islands, the Strait of Gibraltar, and the south coasts of Portugal and Spain.

decided to set sail for home. They still had slaves on board, but they had captured enough gold, silver, and pearls to make the trip a financial success.

Trouble at Sea

The men were sailing back to England when they encountered a terrible storm that threw them off course. Hawkins's fleet now consisted of eight ships. (They had sunk one of the Portuguese ships.) One of the ships was separated from the rest and eventually found its way back to England without the others. But the remaining ships were badly damaged and could not have made it back without repairs. Hawkins decided to sail to the closest port to get the boats fixed.

At this Spanish port, the sailors were on guard. San Juan de Ulua was a small and relatively unimportant town. But they knew that the *flota*, a Spanish fleet that carried goods from the New World to Spain, regularly stopped there on its way back home. The men on the flota were unafraid of combat, and their ships were widely known to be well armed. Hawkins's men hoped to leave the port before they encountered the flota, but after four days, they could see that the flota was approaching. Hawkins wanted to prepare for battle, but he didn't want to strike first. The English sailors got their cannons into position and waited.

The fleet of Drake and Hawkins was moored at San Juan de Ulua in Mexico (then New Spain) during a trading expedition when the Spanish attacked without warning. Only two English vessels escaped, carrying Drake and Hawkins to safety.

When the Spanish ships approached, Hawkins reasoned with the men on board the other ships. He explained that he was there for repairs, and he was willing to leave the land unharmed if they could stay until their ships were ready to make the trip back to England. The Spaniards agreed, and it seemed that things would remain peaceful. But the flota betrayed Hawkins. They felt it was their duty to ensure that Spanish waters were not used by English ships. The attack they planned was meant to catch the English sailors off guard.

Surprise Attack

On September 23, 1568, the Spanish attacked the English vessels using cannons and muskets. The English sailors fought back, but the damage from the attack was great. Cannonballs and musket fire had damaged many of the ships: Some sank, and others were rendered useless. Worse yet, some of the English sailors were captured. Those who weren't enslaved were killed.

The remaining Englishmen gathered the treasure they had collected and set sail again for England on the last two ships. Hawkins was in command of one of the ships, and Drake was put in command of the other. Although Drake was not terribly experienced, Hawkins put his faith in him. But they faced yet more difficulty returning. The ships were overcrowded and the journey was long. Some of the crew died during the voyage, and others asked to be left in the New World, fearing that they would not survive the trip back. Both Drake and Hawkins survived, however. It took them four months to return home. In this time, their anger towards Spain had grown. They were hungry for revenge.

3

DRAKE THE COMMANDER

Now he, Francis Drake, once the penniless younker on a half-derelict coaster, was going to play the part of an admiral of the Queen! He had her commission or, at any rate, an imposing parchment which at appropriate times he flourished, declaring that it was his brief of authority given by the sovereign.
—George Malcolm Thompson, *Sir Francis Drake*

After the fleet returned home, Drake asked the queen for her permission to sail to the Spanish colonies and steal as much as he could. But Queen Elizabeth I did not want to start a war with Spain. The relations between the countries had been troubled, and she did not want to instigate further problems. She turned down Drake's offer.

But he was not content. Defying the queen, Drake set sail for the Caribbean. His master plan was to sail to the New World and capture as much of Spain's treasure as possible. But he planned well, and his goal for the first trip was just to gather intelligence. He did not attack Spain's ships or land. Instead, he kept his cool and sought out the information he needed to ensure that his next voyage would be a grand success.

Back to the Caribbean

In February of 1571 Drake set sail, again for the Caribbean. He took only one ship, the *Swan*. He knew that this voyage might be treacherous, so he prepared for combat. His crew was also prepared.

When a Spanish ship came into sight, Drake and his men attacked. The other ship's men were so frightened by Drake's attack that they fled their own ship. The Englishmen captured all the treasure on the Spanish boat and sailed on. Drake left on board a letter of warning to Spain. In this letter he explained that any Spaniard that surrendered to him or his men would be treated kindly. He also explained that any opposition would result in his crew acting like "devils rather than men." Drake's message was clear: He would be fair to any man who agreed to his rules. Anyone who tried to fight would regret it.

Drake and his men continued on, raiding Spanish vessels and stealing the goods they carried. People living in the Spanish colonies in the New World were terrified of Drake and his men. They sent a letter to King Philip in Spain, begging for protection. Francis Drake was making a name for himself.

Queen Elizabeth I's forty-five-year reign is considered one of the most glorious in English history. She encouraged and funded many voyages of discovery, including those by Drake, Walter Raleigh, and Humphrey Gilbert. These expeditions prepared England for an age of colonization and trade expansion, which Elizabeth herself recognized by establishing the East India Company in 1600. Overall, Elizabeth's shrewd and decisive leadership brought successes to England during a period of danger both at home and abroad. She died on March 24, 1603, having become a legend in her own time.

Philip II ruled Spain from 1556 to 1598. In 1588, persistent attacks by the English on Spanish ships coupled with Philip's desire to overthrow Queen Elizabeth I and take the English throne led him to plan the invasion of England by an armada of 130 ships and 30,000 men. However, some 60 ships were lost and 15,000 men killed. The Spanish Armada was defeated.

The word was out that Drake had stolen a great deal of treasure from the Spanish. Search parties were sent to comb the sea and find him, but they came up with nothing. In June 1571, the Englishmen sailed home. The journey had been a success: Their ship was loaded with valuable cargo. It seemed that Drake had gotten his revenge on the Spanish.

Another Voyage

Although his last trip had been quite successful, Drake wanted to set out to sea again. He knew there was more treasure to be taken, and in May 1572, he was ready to go after it. This trip was bigger than the last, with another ship, the *Pasco*, joining the *Swan* and more men than had previously accompanied Drake. The new ship was much larger than the *Swan* and was outfitted with cannons. Drake's men were prepared for whatever came their way. And with the addition of the *Pasco*, they were able to carry much more cargo than before. There was the possibility that they could return to England with an even greater amount of treasure than in the past.

Setback

Although Francis Drake's voyages were quite successful, the fall of 1572 presented great challenges for Drake and his crew. Disease seized the men, and a total of thirty died. One of the men, Joseph Drake, was Francis's younger brother. Francis's brother John was also killed that year while attempting to capture a Spanish warship.

These coins were issued during the reign of Philip II, king of Spain. Philip was also the king of Naples and Sicily from 1554 to 1598, and, as Philip I, king of Portugal from 1580 to 1598.

The fleet sailed back to the Caribbean to find that their previous hiding place had been discovered. They knew it was not safe to stay there, so they found a new hiding place and got to work building a fort, in case they were faced with battle. While they were working on their new hiding place, an English captain named James Raunse came to them with a proposition. He and Drake had sailed together before, and he wanted to join forces with Drake and his crew. Raunse had captured two Spanish ships, and he and his crew were sailing with them. The addition of the new men and ships pleased Drake. Together, they were bigger and stronger. This gave Drake more confidence in his abilities. He began to formulate a plan.

A Daring Plan

Drake decided to stop raiding Spanish ships and instead focused on gathering treasure from Spanish land instead. He and his men pulled up into Nombre de Dios on the Isthmus of Panama in the middle of the night. They surprised the Spanish by attacking from different sides and capturing the cannons that protected the land. Although the Spanish outnumbered the English, they fled after a brief battle. During this fight, one of the English sailors was killed, and Drake was shot in the leg. Injured and bleeding, he continued on, determined not to let his injury slow him down. But his crew did not feel the same way. Rather than waste time raiding the land for gold and silver, they bandaged his leg and brought him back to his ship. Their captain's life was worth more to them than any amount of treasure.

The plan had failed, but at least Drake was alive. It wasn't long before he recovered, raiding ships and increasing the amount of treasure he and his men had stolen. He also decided to try his plan again, but a little differently

Drake took the Spanish by surprise, not only launching attacks on their ships, but also targeting Spanish towns in the New World. This illustration shows soldiers making off with goods looted from an unfortunate town.

than the previous attempt. Instead of approaching from the water, he wanted to ambush a mule train and attack from the land. But getting on one of these treasure trains proved difficult, and he was unable to do so on his first try.

After his failed attempt, Drake knew that the Spanish expected a land attack, so he purposely continued raiding ships instead of trying the land attack plan again. He wanted the Spanish to think he had given up. But in truth he had not. He was just biding his time until he felt it was safe to try again.

Power in Numbers

Drake had a habit of meeting and joining forces with other groups. For example, he was given valuable information about the treasure trains by a group of men called the Cimarrones. These men were slaves from Africa who had escaped their masters in the Caribbean. They lived together in the jungles of Central America, and their knowledge proved to be a great help to Drake and his men.

Around February 1573, Drake became acquainted with another person whose experience and knowledge were valuable: Guillaume Le Testu. Le Testu was a French sailor, and much like Drake, was an explorer and a pirate. Le Testu was familiar with the area and wanted to pool resources with Drake to pull off a raid of Nombre de Dios. Drake's men, the Cimarrones, and Le Testu's men decided to work together. In April 1573, they made their move.

The men were able to capture over twenty-five tons of precious metals (gold and silver) during the raid of Nombre de Dios. Some of the silver had to be buried because Drake and his men had to act fast and couldn't carry so much at once. All in all, the raid was very profitable. They captured goods that would be worth more than $5 million today. But the plan wasn't foolproof. As they tried to escape the land and get back on the ship, they ran into difficulty.

A Tragic End

Drake's vessels were not waiting at the port as he had expected, so he set out on a shoddily built raft to find them. The waters were shark-infested, and Drake's crew wondered if they would ever see their captain again. Luckily, Drake was able to recover the ships and sail back to land to pick up the men who were hiding with the treasure.

Although the Englishmen took away a great deal of valuable goods, the unfortunate consequence of the raid was discovered: Le Testu had been captured and killed by Spanish men looking for the perpetrators of the crime. It was time for the English sailors to head home.

Elizabeth the Great

Queen Elizabeth I led an extraordinary life. She was born in 1533 to Anne Boleyn and Henry VIII, a man who wanted nothing more than to be blessed with the birth of a son. In fact, he wanted a son so badly that he either divorced or beheaded four wives who did not bear him a son. One wife who bore him a son, Edward, died after childbirth. Elizabeth was close to her father, though, and excelled in her studies as a youngster.

Edward was only ten when Henry died, and he ruled for six years before succumbing to tuberculosis in 1553. Elizabeth became ruler of England in 1558, and she kept the throne for nearly half a century. Although it was unusual for a woman to rule a nation, she performed her duties very well. She was respected and honored by those in power in her country and others. Elizabeth's compassion and warm nature helped ensure the welfare of her country and the happiness of the English people. She never married, but counted many men as close friends, including Sir Francis Drake.

In naval matters, Queen Elizabeth was feared and respected. This was mainly due to Drake's piracy, which kept other countries from attempting anything that could be used as a reason for revenge.

Elizabeth died in 1603, but her legacy lives on. She is considered one of the earliest feminists and has been the subject of books, movies, and discussion for years.

Back in England

Drake returned home to England on a Sunday, and church services were interrupted by the news that he was back. Drake had become well known by this time, due to his incredible wealth and bravery. Queen Elizabeth was quite impressed with the great amounts of treasure he had stolen, and she was clearly glad that he had made out so well. But in 1573, England and Spain had reached a point where their relations were friendly. As proud of Drake as the queen was, she could not publicly show her support. Doing so could have started another fight between the two countries, and the queen did not want that.

The next few years of Drake's life are a mystery. It is known that he went to Ireland to help the earl of Essex suppress a rebellion that was about to occur in that country, but not much else is known. It seems that Drake was being patient, waiting until the time was right to set sail once again.

4

THE FAMOUS VOYAGE

Here hence we sailed to a place called Arica, and being entred the port, we found there three small barkes which we rifled, and found in one of them 57 wedges of silver, Each of them weighing about 20 pound weight, and every of these wedges were of the fashion and bignesse of a brickbat.
—E. P. Cheyney, *Readings in English History*

Drake was approached by investors who wanted to help him set sail on another voyage. Drake wanted to explore the Pacific Ocean, which was off-limits to the English at the time. On previous trips to the New World, he had caught glimpses of this magnificent water and had sworn that he would one day sail the Pacific. The time seemed right.

Piracy was, of course, the main goal of this trip. The profits from this voyage were to come from captured Spanish cargoes. And the details of the venture were to be kept secret, in an attempt to keep the Spanish from retaliating.

One particularly noteworthy aspect of this voyage was the use of one of the queen's ships, the *Swallow*. It has been said that the queen also contributed money to the expedition, but that point is debatable. What we are sure of is the queen's support. Drake named his new boat the *Pelican* after Queen Elizabeth's fascination with this kind of bird. All the boats were heavily armed. Drake and his crew were prepared for an attack.

On November 15, 1577, they set out. Their first attempt at sea failed, as nasty weather headed their way and severely damaged one of the ships. The force of the wind was too great, and it knocked one of the ships into the rocks of the harbor in Cornwall. The sailors returned to Plymouth briefly, repaired the injured ships, and headed out once again.

A Second Attempt

By December 13, 1577, Drake and his fleet of five ships were ready to get back on course. Drake's ship, the *Pelican*, was the fleet's flagship. His men also took the *Elizabeth*, the *Marigold*, the *Swan*,

This replica of the *Golden Hind*, the galleon in which Drake circumnavigated the world, is shown sailing into San Francisco Harbor in California. Drake's *Golden Hind* was seventy-five feet long and twenty feet wide, and there was not much room for the seamen. They had to live, eat, and sleep in small spaces which were hardly ever dry. They usually slept on bare boards and had very little apart from the clothes they wore. They lived off salt pork, beef, cheese, dried fish, and biscuits. Without fresh fruit and vegetables, the seamen often had scurvy. This made them tired and kept them from working properly.

and the *Benedict*. The ships sailed out of Plymouth and headed down toward the coast of Africa, much to the confusion of the sailors: Drake had told the men that they would be sailing to the Mediterranean Sea. He kept their destination a secret because he wanted to be sure that no information could be leaked to the Spanish.

On Christmas Day they caught sight of land. Two days later, they anchored their boats at a small island called Mogador, off the coast of Morocco. Here they learned about the local ship traffic from the natives. The crew was able to rest and fish, and a small boat was prepared for the purpose of raiding other boats. They left Mogador unharmed and set sail again, looking for boats to raid.

Drake and his men continued to sail around the coast of Africa, and here they found ships to seize. They added six ships to their fleet, as well as a great deal of captives and riches. But it was too much for Drake to handle. After taking aboard the valuables from the ships, he let the extra boats go, along with the men he had taken.

The next stop was the island of Maio in the Cape Verde Islands off the coast of West Africa, where seventy men were sent ashore to look for valuable goods. But they encountered a land that had already been plundered. The natives of the island had been

This seventeenth-century map shows the route that Drake's expedition took from England to Mogador, off the coast of Morocco.

recently attacked, and the pirates who had raided the island left nothing except some clean water and meat for the Englishmen to take. It was a disappointment for the sailors, who expected to encounter merchant ships with plenty of riches on board to be stolen.

Word of Drake's journey and his reputation was spreading, and people on various lands were preparing for the pirates. The Englishmen were unable to land at Sao Tiago, Cape Verde Islands, because they were being fired at from the island. They were obviously not welcome, so they continued sailing, hoping for better luck elsewhere.

Preparing for the Long Voyage

Upon arriving in the Cape Verde Islands, Drake and his crew seized a Portuguese ship, and some of the men went on board to sail it with the rest of the fleet. They named this boat *Mary*, after Drake's wife, Mary Newman, whom he had married in 1569. They also kept the boat's pilot aboard to steer the ship. The pilot was experienced in the local waters, and his knowledge was very helpful to them. In addition, his ship was large and held useful goods.

They sailed with this experienced pilot and his crew for a while but were unable to stop anywhere to pick up supplies as they had hoped. It would have been risky to dock the boat at Fogo, where there was an active volcano.

At Brava, the vessels encountered a coastline whose rocky waters they were not equipped to handle. Drake made an important decision. He let go of the Portuguese captives, giving them just enough food and water to survive the trip back in the small boat he gave them. The commander was kept on to help them steer their vessels.

Although they had not acquired the supplies they desired, the men kept sailing toward the Strait of Magellan, a widely unused passage between the Atlantic and Pacific at the bottom of South America. On the long trip, however, Drake ran into personal difficulties with his dear friend, Thomas Doughty. It has been documented that Doughty caught Drake's brother, Thomas, stealing goods from the Portuguese ship. When Doughty reported the theft, Drake was enraged. He did not believe Doughty and made no attempt to hide his anger. He felt that the accusation was disrespectful to both Drake brothers. Tension between Doughty and Drake would continue to grow as they sailed across the Atlantic.

It was a long journey, and the heat and lack of provisions worked against the men. They sailed for weeks without sighting land. Men who were usually calm became frustrated and unhappy. Tempers began to flare, and some of the men stopped getting along. Doughty and Drake especially were at odds, each trying to gather unfavorable information about the other. Doughty had been in command of one of the ships, but Drake

Het Derde Nau

Capo Iu...
Elifabeths Baÿ
Mefdel Baÿ

Pinguyns
Eÿlanden

Het twede
Nau

t'Hoorfte Nau

M A R

D E L

N O R

T

R I

This is a map of the Strait of Magellan, which was discovered in
1520 by another great explorer, Ferdinand Magellan of Portugal,
who also attempted the first circumnavigation of the globe. Magellan
named the strait the "Channel of All Saints," but it eventually came
to be known by the name of its discoverer. The Strait is 330 miles
long and ranges from 2.5 to 15 miles wide. It separates Tierra del
Fuego and other islands from the rest of South America. The strait
was important in the days of sailing ships, especially before the
Panama Canal was built, and is still used by ships rounding South
America. One of the most scenic waterways in the world, it affords
an inland passage protected from almost continuous ocean storms.

DVS FVEGO

MAR DEL

Ridders Baÿ

Mauritio

d'Ongheluckige Baÿ
Besloten Baÿ
De Sorchlijcke Reede
gena empt de Clip-
pe Baÿ

Z uÿd-hoeck

ME

CÆ

PARS

ZVR

SCALA

Germanicarum Milliarium.

1 2 3 4 5 6 7 8 9 10 11 12 13 14 15

removed him from the prestigious position. Doughty spent his time trying to instigate a revolt against Drake. He was eventually found out by Drake and was later put in front of a jury. Doughty was found guilty and executed for his offense.

Continuing On

On August 24, 1578, Drake's ships entered the Strait of Magellan. Their supplies nearly depleted, they stopped at an island with a large population of penguins. With no other way to replenish their food supply, the men killed many birds and used them for food. They also came upon a group of islands that had previously been undiscovered. It is not known for certain how many islands they took possession of, but it was largely believed that three islands were discovered and that they were named Elizabeth (for the queen), Bartholomew, and Saint Georges.

By this time, Drake and his men were sailing with a fleet of three ships. The *Swan* and the *Mary* had been destroyed because there were not enough men to work on all the ships. The sailors prepared themselves for the dangerous trip through the Strait of Magellan, whose waters were known to be rocky and shallow in places. It would be a long journey, and the men were unsure of what to expect. They held a short ceremony, during which Drake renamed the *Pelican*. He decided to call it the *Golden Hind*.

Magellan's Voyage Around the World

Ferdinand Magellan is often credited with leading the first circumnavigation of the globe, or voyage to sail around the world. The entire trip lasted from 1519 until 1522, but Magellan was killed in the Philippines in 1521, leaving his crew to finish the voyage without him.

Magellan's voyage was much like Francis Drake's. Members of Magellan's crew tried to turn the rest of the men against him, and they were found out and executed. But there were still more forces working against Magellan.

A battle with the people of the Philippine Islands proved to be the end of Magellan's life. After sailing so far and learning such important information, he was killed before he could complete his journey. The credit for circumnavigating the globe was given to Juan Sebastian Elcano. Magellan's importance was later recognized, and today we generally credit him for undertaking the first trip around the world.

It is undeniable, however, that Magellan was the first navigator to cross the Pacific from east to west. He also helped to disprove the common belief that the East Indies was a short voyage by ship from the New World.

The trip through the strait took them only fourteen days. They surged through the dangerous waters, excited but nervous about reaching the Pacific. As they sailed into the sea they encountered horrendous weather. For almost two months, the ships were blown by the wind and tossed in the storm. To make matters worse, the maps they used showed an incorrect coastline. They sailed northwest, hoping to find land that would serve as shelter from the storm. But all they found was the open sea.

Scurvy Scare

After battling the horrible storm in 1578, Drake and his crew had another setback. Many men on board the *Golden Hind* were suffering from a disease called scurvy, which made the sailors very ill.

Scurvy is caused by a lack of vitamins from fresh fruit and vegetables in a person's diet. The men who sailed on the *Golden Hind* had gone for a long time without these necessary vitamins (specifically vitamin C) and were suffering for it. Symptoms of scurvy include swollen and painful gums, loose teeth, and easily bruised skin. It is a painful illness, and many of the sailors suffered greatly. Some of the men even died from this disease.

The weather made it impossible to sail well. Drake and his men tried to find land but could not. One night the storm was so bad that the *Marigold* sank, killing all the men aboard. The stormy weather also blew the *Elizabeth* and the *Golden Hind* away from each other one night. The two boats could not find each other, and the captain of the *Elizabeth* decided to sail back to England after a lengthy attempt at finding Drake and his ship. This meant that Drake, in command of the *Golden Hind*, was out at sea without any other boats or crew. His ship sailed the Pacific without any other English vessels.

But this part of the trip was not a complete disaster. Drake proved that a continent called Terra Australis, a continent that Magellan had claimed to be located at the tip of South America, was not where Magellan had claimed. It was Drake's discovery that if Terra Australis existed at all, it was farther south. Drake's hypothesis was only partially true. We now know that Terra Australis does not actually exist. But journeys like those of Magellan and Drake helped determine the correct geographical locations of lands and seas on the globe.

5

FINDING RICHES

June 17, 1579

In 38 deg. 30 min. We fell in with a fit and convenient harbor and June 17, came to anchor there, where we stayed till the 23 July. During all which time, not withstanding it was the height of summer, we were continually visited with nipping cold, neither could we at any time within a fourteen day period find the air so clear as to be able to take height the sun or stars.
—Francis Drake, *The World Encompassed*

On October 28, 1578, Drake and his men decided to sail north, and they stopped in Chile. By this time, Drake's crew had dwindled from 170 men to only about 80. Many men had died during the trip through the strait, and others were killed in battle. The loss of men was significant.

A ship burns in the harbor at Valparaiso as Dutch and Spanish troops contest the newly conquered coast of Chile in this image by Theodor de Bry. De Bry is best known for chronicling the earliest European expeditions to the Americas. De Bry, a Flemish goldsmith, engraver, printseller, and bookseller, started the project in 1590. De Bry's work brought to the European public the first images of the exotic world opened up across the Atlantic Ocean by explorers, conquerors, and settlers.

Val Paryſa.

Chile was known for its rich supply of gold. The Englishmen expected to meet resistance from the natives, but the people who lived on the coast of Chile were friendly. The sailors thought they had found allies. They were allowed to trade for fresh food. But then things took a turn for the worse. The natives attacked and killed four of the men. Others were wounded, including Drake, who was hit twice in his head (once in the eye!) with an arrow. All of the men who fought in this battle were injured, and two were held captive and never retrieved. They left Chile in search of a place where they would be safe.

The men stopped at various Spanish settlements as they sailed on. They captured some treasure but had not found a place with an enormous amount of riches to take back to England. They also encountered resistance and fought a minor battle with the residents of one small Spanish town. It seemed that people were prepared for the English pirates, because the men were met with great hostility at many of the places they stopped. They found success on February 28, when they caught a group of Spanish sailors off guard and boarded their ship. On this ship they found valuable goods such as food, gold, silver, and other things of worth. They also captured the ship and found that it was faster than the *Golden Hind*. The treasure was plentiful, but not nearly as great as what was in store for the sailors.

In Search of the Treasure Ship

Drake and his men were searching for a way to capture a lot of treasure at once. When they heard that a treasure ship carrying silver had left Callao, in what is now Peru, three days earlier, they decided to find the ship and steal the goods on board. The person who spotted the ship was to be given a gold chain by Drake as a reward.

Drake's cousin, John, spotted the ship on March 1, 1579. It took a few days for them to catch up with the ship, but when they did, the English raided it and took enormous quantities of silver and gold worth about $7 million today. The battle that ensued was ferocious. Shots were fired from both sides, but the English sailors were able to get on board the treasure ship and take it over.

The men were very pleased with what they had acquired. It was the most treasure they had ever taken from one place. In addition to gold, silver, and jewels, they also obtained supplies for their boats and food for the crew. There was so much that it took several days to get it all on to the *Golden Hind*.

More Success at Sea

Drake had even more success as he sailed along the western coast of Mexico. He and his men raided other ships and captured more goods. One of the ships they captured gave up without a fight! But Drake had to remain cautious, even though his voyage was going well. Drake knew that the Spanish would be looking for them, trying to get back the treasure they had taken, and wanting to get revenge on Drake.

Drake also knew that going back they way they had come would have been a mistake: The Strait of Magellan was dangerous, as they had learned from their initial rocky trip through the strait. In addition, people might have been looking for them there. Drake decided to sail west. He wanted to cross the Pacific and head home. His goal was to travel across the globe to reach his destination.

Important Discoveries

Drake's journeys were not only about capturing various treasures. Although he was very successful in that area, it is important to note that he also helped people to understand where various bodies of water and lands were. During Drake's time, maps were primitive and often simply wrong. Drake's discoveries helped to shape people's under-standing of what the world looked like.

And although Drake did discover new lands, he also helped to clarify geographical rumors. At this time, it was believed that there was a northwest pas-sageway through Central America and North America. Drake sailed north until he realized that there was no such passageway.

One of Drake's other discoveries was an area near present-day San Francisco, California. Drake and his men ended up there on June 17, 1579, and Drake claimed the land for England, calling it New Albion. They docked the boat there for repairs, and some of the men went to explore the area. They also gathered food and fresh water to take back on the *Golden Hind*. Drake planned the rest of their voyage using maps he had taken from Spanish ships. They were sailing the Pacific Ocean, which was off-limits to the English, and these maps were especially helpful.

Drake Conquers the Spice Trade

Out in the ocean, the sailors spent sixty-eight days without even glimpsing land. The first bit of land they saw was the Philippines. However, they did not stop here. They kept going until they reached the Spice Islands (now known as the Moluccas, of the republic of Indonesia), which were known for the exportation of expensive and rare spices. The Spice Islands were under Portuguese control, but the ruler of the land wasn't happy with the arrangement. The Sultan of Ternate agreed to meet with Drake to discuss the possibility of a better trade arrangement between England and the Spice Islands. In the end, Drake proved successful again. He sailed away knowing that England was to receive exclusive trade rights in exchange for helping free the Spice Islands from Portuguese control.

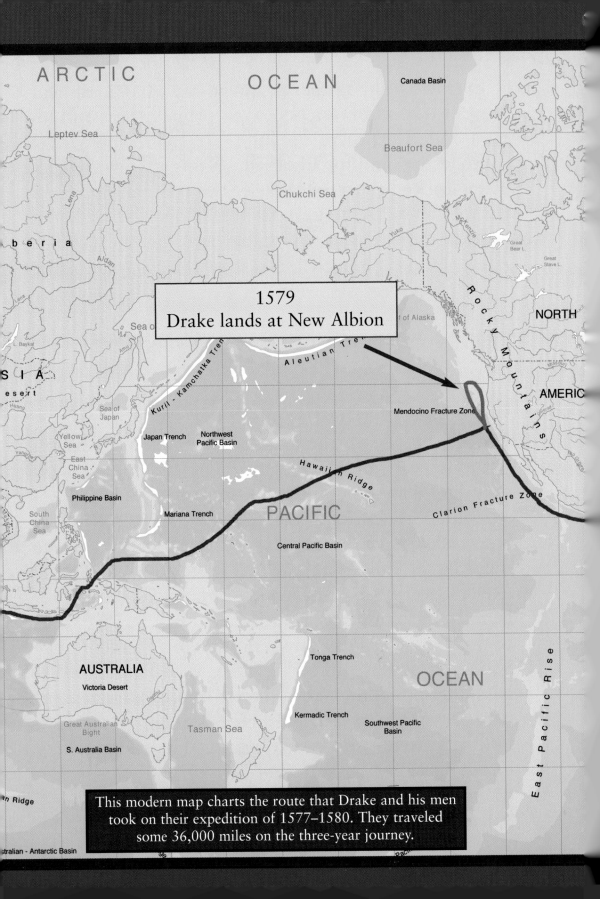

1579
Drake lands at New Albion

This modern map charts the route that Drake and his men took on their expedition of 1577–1580. They traveled some 36,000 miles on the three-year journey.

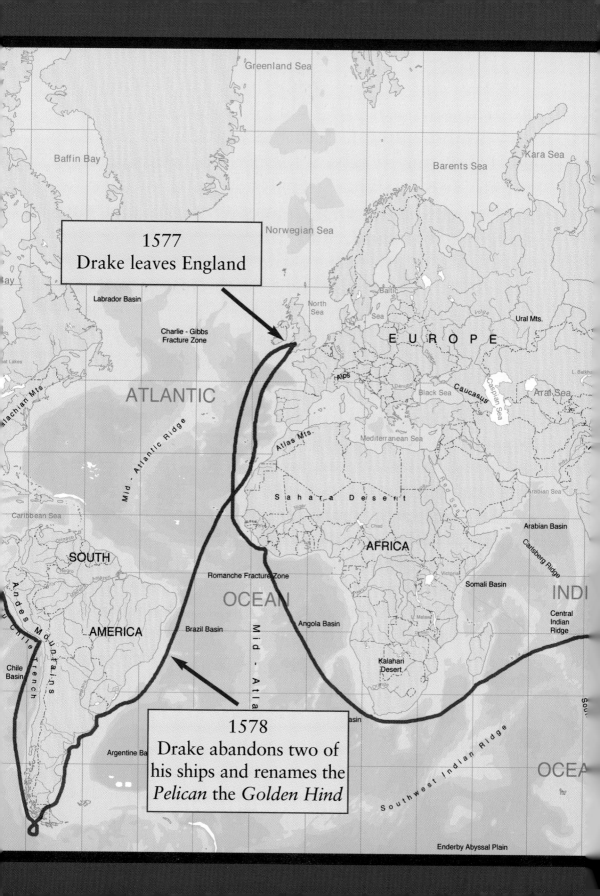

1577
Drake leaves England

1578
Drake abandons two of
his ships and renames the
Pelican the *Golden Hind*

Drake sailed away from this land looking for another place for the men to dock for a while. They found a small, deserted island with a good supply of fresh crabs and lobsters. Although it had no fresh drinking water, the island was a good place for the men to stay. Drake named the island Crab Island, and the men lived on the island for a month, while making necessary repairs to the ship. They were safe on Crab Island, as no one knew they were there.

But their good fortune would not last long. The *Golden Hind* crashed into an underwater coral reef that severely damaged the boat. Water flowed on board the ship, and there was a hole in the ship's bottom. They were stuck on the reef and tried to throw cargo overboard to make the boat weigh less, in the hopes it would be easier to sail on. Once free of the reef, the sailors were able to repair the boat and get back on track. But they had lost valuable supplies and needed to stop and pick up more food, firewood, and water for the men on the ship. Without it, they wouldn't last the rest of the journey home.

They were lucky to have found the southern coast of Java, where they were treated well. They stayed there for about two weeks and were able to purchase much needed food. At another stop they were also treated well and stocked up on the food that would last them until their return home. They were fortunate enough to be able to purchase beef and chicken, although at an extremely high price.

The last leg of their journey was an uninterrupted two and a half months of sailing. The men must have been excited about their return home, as they had been gone for a very long time. In this time, they had lost many men to disease, battle, and the cruelty of the sea. But they had gained riches beyond belief, more than England could have hoped for. They were fast approaching their homeland.

6

WEALTH AND FAME

He is served on silver dishes with gold borders and gilded garlands, in which are his arms. He carries all possible dainties and perfumed waters . . . He dines and sups to the music of viols.

—Don Francisco de Zarate, letter to the
viceroy of Mexico, 1579

After sailing through the Indian Ocean and back around Africa, the Englishmen were ready to go home. Their journey had taken almost three years. They had lost ships and lives on their trip. Their boat, the *Golden Hind*, had been battered. On September 26, 1580, Drake and his men sailed into Plymouth harbor after sailing around the globe.

But they didn't know what to expect. For all they knew, in the time they had been gone, England and Spain could have become allies, which would mean that the queen would be forced to persecute the men for what they had done. There were many things to

Upon his return from stealing riches from the Spanish, Drake wasn't sure he would be welcomed by Queen Elizabeth. He worried that the queen would have made amends with her longtime rival, King Philip, and that he would be punished for his piracy.

consider, like whether the queen was even still alive, and the political situation in England. They had to be careful about announcing their return. Drake knew that he was an enemy of Spain. He had raided their ships and invaded their land. He had taken valuable goods and fought battles with Spanish men. At the time, Spain was a very important country. It controlled large parts of the New World, and it was a rich and powerful nation. England was not prepared for a war with Spain. And although Queen Elizabeth secretly approved of Drake's journey, whether she would embrace or punish him was yet to be seen.

Boat Filled with Riches

In the three years of Drake's journey, he and his men had captured many treasures, such as gold, silver, spices, maps, and jewels. Their geographical discoveries were considered as valuable as riches. Drake was the only living person to have completed a journey around the globe. He was suddenly a very important and wealthy man, but he had to be cautious before stepping back on English soil.

Drake did not want his crew to panic at the thought of not being welcome back home. So he told the men that there was a plague epidemic in Plymouth and that they had to stay on the boat so he could assess the situation. In truth, there actually was an outbreak of the plague, but this was not the reason they were ordered to stay on the boat. Drake sent a secret message to the queen and waited for her reply to see how he should proceed. He described in the letter all the treasures they had brought back and the discoveries he wanted to share with her. In the meantime, the sailors stayed on the boat, waiting for orders from Drake. They docked at an island that is now known as Drake's Island. While they awaited their fate, Drake's wife, Mary, heard of their arrival and came to visit Drake, as did the mayor of Plymouth.

Luckily, the queen agreed to meet with Drake at the royal court. When they met, Drake told her of the things he had seen and lands he had discovered in her name. During their six-hour discussion, Drake explained that a lot of what he had stolen was treasure that had not been registered with Spain, meaning that the owners could not report it. This also meant that the Spanish government had no way of knowing exactly how much was plundered. Although Spain had requested earlier that England return all the goods that Drake had stolen, Queen Elizabeth was so impressed with Drake that she refused. She defied their trust, and Spain was angry. The king of Spain demanded that Drake be killed.

The Royal Visit

On April 1, 1581, the queen visited the *Golden Hind* in London. The boat was taken ashore as a permanent memorial to Drake's voyage, and there was to be a banquet to celebrate. The boat was in fine shape, with colorful sails replacing the old ones, and decorations celebrating England. The crew was on its best behavior for this visit.

The queen had a sword in hand as Drake knelt before her. According to Harry Kelsey's *Sir Francis Drake: The Queen's Pirate*, she declared for all to hear, "My royal brother, the King of Spain, has demanded your head. We shall ask Monsieur to be the headsman." She handed the sword to the French nobleman at her side. He tapped Drake's shoulders with the blade and declared Drake a knight of England. "Arise, Sir Knight, the master thief of the unknown world," he said. Drake stood, knowing that he was officially thanked for his hard work. His future was no longer uncertain. The queen had recognized him as an vital force in her community.

Drake then presented the queen with gifts from his journey, and a grand affair ensued. The people on the ship celebrated with the distinguished guests.

Queen Elizabeth I knights Francis Drake on the deck of the *Golden Hind* at Deptford, London, after his round-the-world voyage. In the past, knights were professional warriors, but by Drake's time, knighthood had come to signify a social honor. Today, knighthood remains a form of recognition for significant contributions to English national life, and modern-day recipients have included politicians, actors, scientists, and businesspeople.

Political Fame

Sir Francis Drake had completed an expedition around the world, and now he was ready to take on the role of political figure in England. He was elected to Parliament, the law-making body in England, and he was given the honor of serving on a board that oversaw the nation's naval duties. But his sailing life was not completely over. In 1584, Drake was asked to deal with an unfavorable situation in the English Channel. Dutch pirates were attacking English ships, and Drake was called in to help.

But this time was not all happiness for Drake. Soon after Drake was finally reunited with his beloved wife, Mary, she died in January of 1583.

A Second Marriage

After Drake's first wife, Mary, passed away, he sought out a second wife. In 1585, Drake married Elizabeth Sydenham, a woman much younger than he. Sydenham was from a distinguished and wealthy family in England. It has been noted that she was intelligent, attractive, and possessed fine manners.

They had been married since 1569, and her death dealt Drake quite a blow. In addition, Drake was not liked by all in England. Many thought of him as a thief and didn't like the methods by which he earned his wealth. One of these men was John Doughty, the brother of Thomas Doughty, whom Drake had had executed for trying to turn his men against him. John Doughty accused Drake of being a murderer and was insistent that Drake be punished for the murder of his brother. Doughty ended up in prison for plotting against Drake.

Drake's Generosity

Drake's newfound wealth enabled him to give lavish presents. He had become a good friend of the queen and often showered her with very expensive gifts, such as a diamond cross and a crown encrusted with emeralds. But many did not appreciate this generosity. It was said that he only gave gifts to those who were influential, and that he was trying to buy power.

It was also noted that Drake was not very generous with his crew, the men who had worked so hard for him. They were promised riches while on their journey, but once they returned they were given only enough to live on. Meanwhile, Drake was one of the wealthiest men in England.

It seems that Drake was cautious about who he gave money and treasures to. It was easy for Drake to buy off enemies, but many respected men in England wanted nothing to do with him. Many did not want to accept stolen goods and did not respect Drake for the way he earned his wealth. His piracy was looked down on by many, and this was a continuing problem throughout his life.

Nevertheless, Drake was a very important man, one who was in good favor with the queen. Although he had obtained the fame he desired in England, his sailing days were not over. England still considered him to be an important sailor and explorer, and his presence was requested on various journeys.

7

LATER VOYAGES

But the Sailors were foe far from being daunted by the Number and Strengthe of the Enemie, that as foon as they were difcerned from the top maft–Head, acclamations of Joy refounded through the whole Fleete.
—The English Mercurie, July 23, 1588

After Drake's incredible trip around the world, many plans for other trips were made. Most of these trips were cancelled, however, due in part to Queen Elizabeth's reluctance to let Drake go. They had become good friends, and Drake was the queen's favorite pirate.

In 1585, Drake set sail with about twenty-four ships and eight smaller boats. Drake's mission was to cause as much damage to Spain as possible. Relations between England and Spain were not good once again, and the queen trusted Drake to take down the Spanish overseas empire. It was the first time that Drake was in charge of such a large fleet of ships.

The West Indies

After sailing for about three and a half months, with stops in various towns on the Cape Verde Islands and the West Indies, Drake decided to surprise the town of Santo Domingo, in Hispaniola, (modern-day Haiti and Dominican Republic), and attack it. There were guards posted at this town to ensure the safety of its residents and protect them from attacks like the ones Drake had built his career on. The Englishmen entered from the jungle, surprising the Spanish force that defended the city. Drake's ships also fired cannons from the sea as an extra defense against the Spanish army. The English were triumphant.

Drake and his sailors stayed on Hispaniola for about three weeks, during which time they drove the residents away and searched the land for things of value to take back on the ship. When asked how much it would take for the English to leave, Drake asked for an impossible sum of money. Hispaniola was once a prosperous island, but it had seen better days and did not have the treasures that Drake wanted. It took much negotiation, but the people of Hispaniola contributed what they could, and the Englishmen went on their way to Cartagena.

This picture of Nombre de Dios comes from the *Histoire Naturelle des Indes*, which is known as the "Drake Manuscript."

Drake's Relationship with His Captive

While in Cartagena, Drake took a hostage. He needed a hostage so that he could request a ransom in exchange for the man's life. This hostage was named Alonso Bravo, and Drake stayed with him in his house during the negotiations. The two men became close friends during this time, which seems a highly unlikely scenario. But they spent many hours talking, and Drake even allowed Bravo to travel to another estate to be with his dying wife.

Bravo's wife died during his time as a prisoner, and her burial in Cartagena was attended by many, including Drake. But Drake, always thinking about business, demanded more money from Bravo than was expected. The only consideration Drake made was a decrease in the sum he wanted, due to his host's great hospitality.

Cartagena was a small town that did not have a military to defend itself. Nonetheless, when the authorities there heard that Drake might be arriving, they took extra precautions to guard against the men. But their precautions were not enough. In the middle of the night on February 10, Drake's men attacked. The fight was short-lived, however. Drake's men overpowered the defenders of Cartagena, but not without their fair share of losses. Different records indicate various amounts of casualties, but at least a hundred English sailors and soldiers lost their lives. Some of these men died fighting and others died of disease during the weeks they stayed, negotiating ransom payments.

Leaving Cartagena

Drake's fleet left Cartagena with bars of gold and silver and a number of slaves. Many of the men on the trip wanted to sail home. They thought that they should be happy with what they had received, and were afraid that the Spanish were after them. But before sailing home, they sailed to the East Coast of North America. Drake's men attacked Saint Augustine in present-day Florida on May 28 and 29, 1586, and destroyed the town. They were attacked by the Spanish and lost one of their men, Captain Anthony Powell, who was Drake's sergeant major. They then sailed to Virginia to meet with English colonists who were badly in need of supplies. Unfortunately, Drake and his men had none to spare.

OPIDVM § Augustini liquide nibhes confractum, magnificae habuit bartas, ipsíg solo foecundissimo uctor vero cum inde felicissimae ciuitas ipus in tinerae violatiом. Praesidium ter erat in Hispani selinolg, utro eadem numero et eiusdem Sapien maris Vmbra locatur in loco § Holmus ducte, bas non gra falá quocundrachem pout insgnolepi un aña amplisa bilispitia tenui est ad proebidendae Anglú et Gallос ac uluvestini regionum quia praestat viribus gerit, comparaent

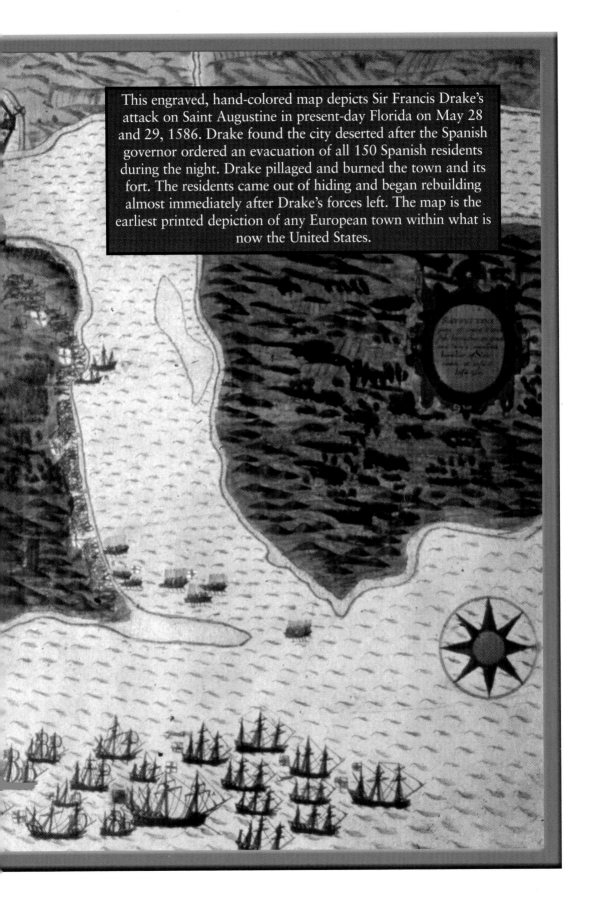

This engraved, hand-colored map depicts Sir Francis Drake's attack on Saint Augustine in present-day Florida on May 28 and 29, 1586. Drake found the city deserted after the Spanish governor ordered an evacuation of all 150 Spanish residents during the night. Drake pillaged and burned the town and its fort. The residents came out of hiding and began rebuilding almost immediately after Drake's forces left. The map is the earliest printed depiction of any European town within what is now the United States.

On July 29, 1586, the men returned to Plymouth. The investors were unhappy, as Drake had not returned with as much treasure as was hoped for. But now England was officially a threat to Spain. Spain's King Philip II was embarrassed by his inability to stop Drake, and he was fearful of Drake's power. Spain had once been a wealthy and powerful nation, while England was small and did not have the influence that Spain did. Now England had found Spain's weaknesses, and Drake was responsible.

King Philip II Retaliates

King Philip II was preparing a fleet of ships to use against the English naval force. His plan was to crush the English navy and then attack England, as Drake had done to his lands many times over. When the English found out about this, they began to prepare for the attack. Drake was put in charge of the fleet of ships that were assembled. In March 1587, the fleet sailed out. It was the largest fleet that Drake had ever commanded, with twenty-four large ships and 3,000 men. Their goal was to intercept the Spanish ships, disarm them, and ensure that they would not be able to reach England to do damage.

Drake's men sailed to Cadiz, a Spanish port that held supplies for the Spanish Armada. Ships were captured or destroyed, as were weapons, supplies, and food. If the Spanish

Residents of an English coastal city light beacons to warn of the approach of the Spanish Armada.

intended to stop here to load up on things they needed for their trip, they would be out of luck. Drake's next stop was the coast of Portugal, where the Englishmen destroyed almost fifty ships. In addition, the Englishmen blockaded the area where the Spanish Armada was preparing for battle. After the Englishmen left Portugal, the Spanish could not get in or out of the harbor there. As a final insult before returning to England, Drake captured a Spanish ship that was loaded with treasure. Although the goal of this mission was to stop the Spanish from attacking, the addition of this Spanish treasure was a welcome victory.

The Armada Returns

King Philip II's assault had been put on hold, but his plan was not over yet. In May 1588, the armada set sail again, ready to attack England. There were 19,000 soldiers, and about 130 boats of various sizes. The fleet that England had prepared to fight back was much smaller, but better armed. Drake was named second in command during this mission. Lord Howard of Effingham (later earl of Nottingham) was in charge.

As the Spanish ships were sailing toward England, a group of English ships was able to sneak up behind them without being noticed. During the first day of the battle, both sides were fairly equal. The Spanish ships could not get close enough to the English ships to capture them, but the English ships were too far for their cannons to reach the Spanish. The Spanish also encountered unusually bad luck when one ship caught fire and another was so badly damaged that it fell behind the others and was captured by the Englishmen.

This illustration depicts the menacing Spanish Armada on its journey to England. Drake's conquests were not the only reason that King Philip II wanted to invade England. He also wished to conquer the English, who were of the Protestant faith, so he could forcibly convert them to Catholicism. In addition to personal animosities towards England's Queen Elizabeth I, Philip II hoped that eliminating Spain's major sea-going rival would boost the Spanish economy.

The admiral of the Spanish Armada surrenders his sword and his ship to Francis Drake. The defeat of the Spanish Armada marked the turning point between the era of Spanish world domination and the rise of England to international supremacy. This battle began the decline of Spain and the ascent of England—it was an event that altered the future of nations and the world.

The Battle of Gravelines was the last straw. Terrible weather conditions forced the Spanish fleet to scatter, and it was unable to regroup and try again. As a result, about 1,500 Spanish sailors were killed and many more were taken hostage. By the time the armada returned home, it had lost about 15,000 men and 60 ships. Once again, the Spanish had been defeated. Sir Francis Drake was now easily the most famous man in England. But the hero was not ready to pack it in. He still had some more exploring to do, and was eager to set out to sea again.

8

THE LEGACY OF SIR FRANCIS DRAKE

But whereas it is most certain that the King doth not only make speedy preparation in Spain, but likewise expecteth a very great fleet from the Straits and divers other places to join with his forces to invade England, we purpose to set apart all fear of danger, and by God's furtherance to proceed by all good means that we can devise to prevent their coming.
—Francis Drake, letter to Mr. Foxe, April 27, 1587

D rake's role in England's success ensured his power over the Spanish. Drake spent some time with his second wife, Elizabeth, before he set out to sea again. His journeys had made him a powerful and well-respected man, and there was no shortage of parties and events for the Drakes to attend. But Drake needed to get out on the sea.

The next expedition Drake dared to take was another journey where the main purpose was to steal goods from Spain. He realized that the coast of Spain was unguarded as the Spanish Armada was still sailing back to Lisbon. By beating the Spanish back to their land, the English sailors would be able to travel there and get on land without fear of attack.

Lisbon Under Attack

The boats set sail in April 1589. Drake was the sea commander, and a man named Sir John Norris was appointed the commander of land forces. Drake believed that they would find the armada at the town of Coruña, Spain. After five days at sea, they reached a deserted town that showed signs that the armada had been there recently. They recognized one ship as definitely having been part of the armada.

They were able to dock at the empty harbor and make their way onto the land. Several thousand soldiers were sent into the town to investigate the land. What they found was that the upper part of the town was heavily guarded by soldiers and a high wall. When an attempt was made to destroy the wall with a mine, the plan backfired and the English suffered under the force of the explosion. Then, using cannons, they tried to break the wall, but many men were crushed by falling rocks as they attempted to enter the highly guarded area. The Englishmen were in trouble, a fate they were not accustomed to at all, considering the success of their earlier expeditions.

After the defeat of the Spanish Armada, Drake returned to sea, but his glory days were over: His joint sea-and-land attack on Lisbon was a shambles. Queen Elizabeth was so angry at his failure that Drake was not employed again for five years, during which time he became mayor of Plymouth and represented the city in Parliament.

Royal Wrath

Queen Elizabeth was very angry with Drake and Norris over the outcome of the Lisbon expedition. She had high expectations of Drake because he had done so well in the past and their relationship was strong. What could Drake have done to anger the queen so much?

The queen was angered that the sailors had sailed a different course than Drake and Queen Elizabeth had agreed upon. She believed they had never intended to go to Santander, Spain, where they were supposed to attack the Spanish. In turn, Drake and Norris claimed that the wind threw them off course and that their advisers told them it was not safe to travel there. Queen Elizabeth was also angry with them for the way they handled the Lisbon situation.

But the queen was especially mad at Drake for allowing the disaster to occur. Many witnesses claimed that it was obvious that many of the soldiers were weakened by disease and unable to fight. Many believed that Drake could have prevented many deaths had he been more cautious about which soldiers were sent to attack.

During the stay in Coruña, many of their weapons were stolen, and men were killed in battle. Much of the food and fresh water was also stolen. The trip was a disaster. Many men lost their lives, and many ships were abandoned or ruined. Disease spread through the ships. When the men returned from their trip, the queen was very displeased. She accused Drake and Norris of failing to obey her commands. She claimed that much of the disaster and lost sailors would have been prevented if the men had followed her orders. The men defended themselves, but left doubt as to their leadership abilities.

Fallen Out of Favor

Drake had been a respected and talented sailor. Much of England loved and appreciated his naval expertise. But his reputation had diminished somewhat. Some people accused him of being cowardly in his actions. Others thought he was just stubborn and too proud. But although the queen had been angry with him, she had not given up on him. They were still friends, and Drake was called on to help when the English got word that the Spanish were coming to attack.

Drake's advice was to ensure that Plymouth harbor was well guarded. The additions of cannons and guns were most likely due to Drake's belief that England needed the extra artillery. The project was expensive and money had to

Privateers such as Sir Francis Drake *(right)* and Sir John Hawkins challenged the Spanish claim to the New World and its riches. The success of their voyages encouraged others who, desperate to become rich, may have acted more like pirates than privateers, and did not restrict their attacks to Spanish ships.

come from somewhere. Many wealthy landowners were recruited to provide money. Drake was one of the men who funded the construction.

During this expensive and lengthy process Drake was named deputy lieutenant for the district, and one of his new responsibilities was to oversee the harbor defenses and ensure that fire ships were built and ready for action. But it wasn't long before Drake was back at sea again, fighting the Spanish. A new expedition was being planned and Drake was prepared to fight again.

The Last Journey

Queen Elizabeth, John Hawkins, and Sir Francis Drake put a lot of money into the next journey. The queen also volunteered six of her ships for the trip. Drake and Hawkins were sharing the responsibility of commanding the fleet—something that neither man was accustomed to. There were 2,500 men sailing on this journey, and it puzzled them that both Drake and Hawkins would be leading them. Both in their fifties, neither was in good physical shape any longer. And more important, each thrived on power. How would they share the authority now that they were both in charge?

The fleet sailed out of Plymouth on August 28, 1595. Almost immediately, Drake and Hawkins were at odds. Drake realized that there were not enough provisions on his

The loss of 15,000 soldiers and 60 ships in the 1588 battle was a huge blow to Spain. The nation eventually recovered from the loss of its armada and fortified its cities in the New World. This move caused Drake and Hawkins's 1595 expedition to America to be a disaster.

ship for all of his men and asked Hawkins to take some of the burden. When Hawkins refused to accept Drake's men, more fighting ensued. Drake and Hawkins disagreed on whether or not they should stop for more supplies. Drake won and the men stopped at the island of Gran Canaria. Unfortunately, the water was too high for the men to get off the boats. A landing was attempted, but failed, resulting in the loss of four men.

When they tried to land on the other side of the island, many Englishmen were killed by natives. Some were taken hostage. Drake and Hawkins decided to leave and sail to the West Indies as they had planned.

Revenge on the English

The Englishmen stopped their boats at Guadeloupe on October 29, 1595. When the men thought they saw English ships sailing towards them, they were very mistaken. They had no idea it was Spanish ships that were coming toward them. One of their ships was captured, and the men on it were taken hostage. The Englishmen were in trouble again.

The men began preparing for a fight. They stayed in Guadeloupe for ten days, bringing guns on to the decks of the ships. But one night trouble found them. Drake was sitting down for dinner when shots were fired into the cabin where he was eating. He was unharmed, but two other men were killed. The sailors took this as a

This image depicts the burial at sea of Sir Francis Drake, marking the end of the life and career of one of the great men of English history. He carried the English flag around the world and helped put the island nation on the road to becoming the worldwide superpower of the time.

sign that they should move on, so they left in search of a safer place to anchor their ships.

Drake Meets His End

The journey was not going well, and the Spanish seemed to be one step ahead of Drake and his men at every turn. They found abandoned towns where they expected to find riches. Even the weather worked against them. Worst of all, a horrible illness was sweeping through the ships, and Drake had caught it. He commanded the ships from his sickbed, as he made up a last will and testament. Sir Francis Drake died on January 28, 1596. His body was put in a lead coffin and buried at sea, against his wishes to be buried on land. An elaborate ceremony was held to honor Sir Francis Drake and his incredible life at sea.

The Death of John Hawkins

John Hawkins, whom Drake had known for so long, fell ill and passed away during this last expedition with Drake. His death on November 12 , 1595, was a great blow to the men aboard the ships, for they had lost a commander and a worthy seaman.

Drake's luck had finally run out. His last journey was a failure, due in part to a lack of discipline after both commanders had lost their lives. The Englishmen encountered more and more difficulties before sailing back to England without much to show for themselves. Not only had they lost both commanders, they had also lost many men.

Sir Francis Drake is a legend, a man whose sailing expertise helped him become one of the most famous men of his time. He raised himself up from the poverty of his childhood to acquire so much money that he was asked to give financial help to his country. His life goal, it seemed, was to ensure distress to the Spanish and King Philip, in particular. His acts of piracy made him a national sensation and placed him in the good favor of Queen Elizabeth, a powerful woman who offered Drake her friendship. His journeys took him far and wide, to places where no one from the Western world had ever been. His discoveries were of great help to his country, and his excellence is still noted to this day. Sir Francis Drake was a king of the seas, a loyal man, of whom England was surely proud.

CHRONOLOGY

1540 It is estimated that Francis Drake is born in March or February in Tavistock, England.

1553 Drake is sent away to work on a ship where he learns to sail and eventually becomes the ship's master.

1566 Drake is appointed second in command on a Hawkins family voyage to the New World.

1567 John Hawkins invites Drake on a journey to sail on the *Jesus of Lubeck*. During this journey, he is put in command of the *Judith*, a fifty-ton ship.

1571 Against Queen Elizabeth's orders, Drake sails to the Caribbean to steal as much Spanish treasure as possible.

1577   On December 13, Drake sets out on his most famous voyage.

1580   On September 26, Drake and his men return with riches from their journey around the world.

1585   Drake sets sail with a fleet of twenty-four ships and defeats the Spanish Armada for the queen of England.

1595   On August 28, Drake sets sail on what was to be his last voyage.

1596   Drake dies at sea on January 28.

GLOSSARY

apprentice A person who serves another in order to learn a skill or trade in return.

armada A large fleet of ships.

circumnavigation To sail completely around the world.

dwindle To waste away.

feminist A person who believes that men and women deserve equal treatment.

fleet A number of warships sailing under one command.

horrendous Especially bad; dreadful.

hospitality The generous and courteous treatment of guests.

musket A large gun, similar to a rifle, that is carried over the shoulder.

navigation The science that deals with getting a boat, plane, or car from one place to another.

opposition Action that is contrary or hostile.

perpetrator The person who carries out a crime.

piracy The act of robbery at sea.

plunder To steal goods using force.

preacher A person who delivers a religious sermon.

primitive Being simple or unsophisticated; relating to an outdated idea.

privateer The commander or one of the crew of such a ship authorized by a government during wartime to attack and capture enemy vessels.

provisions A stock of necessary materials, such as food and water.

raid A surprise attack.

ransom Compensation paid for the return of someone or something.

scurvy A disease caused by lack of vitamin C.

FOR MORE INFORMATION

In the United States

The Mariners' Museum
100 Museum Drive
Newport News, VA 23606
(757) 596-2222
Web site: http://www.mariner.org

Maritime Park Association
P.O. Box 470310
San Francisco, CA 94147-0310
(415) 561-6662
Web site: http://www.maritime.org

In Canada

Maritime Museum of the Atlantic
1675 Lower Water Street, 3rd Floor
Halifax, NS B3J 1S3
(902) 424-7890
Web site: http://museum.gov.ns.ca/mma/index.html

Web Sites

Due to the changing nature of Internet links, the Rosen Publishing Group, Inc., has developed an online list of Web sites related to the subject of this book. This site is updated regularly. Please use this link to access the list:

http://www.rosenlinks.com/lee/frdr/

FOR FURTHER READING

Bard, Roberta. *Francis Drake: First Englishman to Circle the Globe*. Danbury, CT: Children's Press, 1992.

Champion, Neil. *Sir Francis Drake*. Des Plains, IL: Heinemann Library, 2001.

Gallagher, Jim. *Sir Francis Drake and the Foundation of a World Empire*. Broomall, PA: Chelsea House Publishers, 2000.

Henty, G.A. *Under Drake's Flag: A Tale of the Spanish Main*. Mill Hall, PA: Preston-Speed Publications, 1998.

Marrin, Albert. *The Sea King: Sir Francis Drake & His Times*. New York: Simon & Schuster Children's, 1995.

Smith, Alice. *Sir Francis Drake & the Struggle for an Ocean Empire*. Broomall, PA: Chelsea House Publishers, 1993.

BIBLIOGRAPHY

Gallagher, Jim. *Sir Francis Drake and the Foundation of a World Empire*. Broomall, PA: Chelsea House Publishers, 2001.

Kelsey, Harry. *Sir Francis Drake: The Queen's Pirate*. New Haven, CT: Yale University Press, 1998.

Sugden, John. *Sir Francis Drake*. New York: Henry Holt and Company, 1990.

INDEX

A

Africa, 22, 39, 46, 66
Angel, 24

B

Bartholomew Island, 52
Benedict, 45
Boleyn, Anne, 41
Brava, 49
Bravo, Alonso, 78

C

Cadiz, Spain, 82–83
Callao, Peru, 59
cannons, 22, 24, 30, 37, 77, 89, 91
Cape Verde Islands, 22, 46–48, 77
Caribbean/West Indies, 20, 22–30, 31–37, 39, 77–79, 95–98
Cartagena, Colombia, 77–79
Central America, 37–40, 39, 60
Chile, 56–58

Cimarrones, 39, 40
circumnavigation of globe, 5–6, 53, 66, 68, 75
Cornwall, England, 45
Coruña, Spain, 89–91
Crab Island, 64

D

de Castellanos, Miguel, 24
Doughty, John, 73
Doughty, Thomas, 49–52, 73
Drake, Edmund (father), 13, 14
Drake, Francis
    attacks on Spain/Spanish settlements, 33–34, 37–39, 40, 60, 66, 69, 75, 77, 79, 87, 89–91, 95–98
    in California, 61
    in Cape Verde Islands, 22, 46–48, 77
    in Caribbean/West Indies, 20, 22–30, 31–37, 77–79, 95–98
    in Central America, 37–40

circumnavigation of globe,
6, 60, 66, 68, 72, 75
death of, 5, 98
discoveries made, 52, 55,
60–61, 68
early life, 11–19
fame of, 5, 10, 42, 68, 72, 73,
86, 87, 91, 99
first voyages, 14–16
hatred of Spain, 6, 30, 68, 99
injuries suffered, 37, 58
in Ireland, 42
John Hawkins and, 19, 20–30,
93–95
knighthood, 71
last journey, 93–99
in Pacific Ocean, 54–55, 60,
61–64
as pirate, 6, 10, 18, 19, 22,
33–34, 37–39, 40, 43,
46–48, 58–60, 66, 68, 69,
74, 83, 87, 99
in politics, 72, 93
problems experienced, 7–10, 30,
35, 45, 49–52, 54–55, 56–58,
64, 72–74, 89–91, 93–99
Queen Elizabeth and, 6–7, 31,
42, 45, 68, 69, 71, 73, 74,
75, 90, 91, 93, 99
in South America, 25, 52–55,
56–59, 77–79
Spanish Armada and, 82–86
in Spice Islands, 61
uncertainties about, 11, 13, 42
Drake, John (brother), 35
Drake, Joseph (brother), 35
Drake, Thomas (brother), 49
Drake's Island, 69

E

East Indies, 53
Elcano, Juan Sebastian, 5–6, 53
Elizabeth (ship), 45, 55
Elizabeth I, queen of England,
6–7, 31, 41, 42, 45, 66–68,
69, 71, 73, 74, 75, 90, 91,
93, 99
Elizabeth Island, 52
England, relationship with Spain,
6, 19, 22–30, 31, 42, 66,
75, 82–86
English Channel, 72

F

flota, 28–30
Fogo, 48

G

gold, 10, 28, 40, 58, 59, 68, 79
Golden Hind, 52, 54, 55, 58, 59,
61, 64, 66, 71
Gracia Dei, 22
Gran Canaria, 95
Gravelines, Battle of, 86
Guadeloupe, 95

H

Hawkins, John, 19, 20–30,
93–95, 98
Hawkins family, 16–19
Henry VIII, king of England,
14, 41

I

Indian Ocean, 66
Indonesia, 61–64

J

Java, 64
Jesus of Lubeck, 20
jewels, 10, 28, 68, 73
Judith, 22, 24

L

Le Testu, Guillaume, 39–40
Lisbon, Portugal, 87, 90
Lord Howard of Effingham (Earl of Nottingham), 85

M

Magellan, Ferdinand, 5, 53, 55
Magellan, Strait of, 49, 52–54, 56, 60
Maio, 46
Marigold, 45, 55
Mary, 48, 52
Mediterranean Sea, 46
Mexico, 59
Mogador, 46
Moluccas, 61
Morocco, 46
Myllwaye, Anna (mother), 13

N

Netherlands/the Dutch, 72
New Albion, 61
Newman, Mary (first wife), 48, 69, 72–73
New World, 6, 19, 20, 22–28, 30, 31, 33, 43, 53, 68
Nombre de Dios, 37, 40
Norris, Sir John, 89–91
northwest passage, 60

P

Pacific Ocean, 43, 49, 53, 54–55, 60, 61
Panama, Isthmus of, 37
Parliament, 72
Pasco, 35
Pelican (renamed *Golden Hind*), 45, 52
penguins, 52
Philip II, king of Spain, 6, 33, 69, 82, 85, 99
Philippines, 53, 61
piracy, 6, 10, 18, 19, 22, 33–34, 39, 40, 43, 46–48, 58–60, 66, 68, 72
Plymouth, England, 16–18, 45–46, 66, 69, 82, 91, 93
Portugal, 19, 22, 48, 49, 61, 83
Powell, Anthony, 79

R

Raunse, James, 36
Rio de la Hacha, 24

S

Saint Augustine, Florida, 79
Saint Georges Island, 52
San Juan de Ulloa, 28
Santa Marta, Colombia, 25
Santander, Spain, 90
Santo Domingo, Hispaniola, 77
Sao Tiago, Cape Verde Islands, 48
scurvy, 7, 54
silver, 10, 28, 40, 58, 59, 68, 79
Sir Francis Drake: The Queen's Pirate, 71

slaves/slave trade, 19, 22–28, 39, 79

South America, 25, 49, 52–55
    Spain, 6, 7, 19, 22, 69, 82–86, 87, 89–91, 95–99
    relationship with England, 6, 19, 22–30, 31, 42, 66, 75, 82–86

Spanish Armada, 82–86

Spice Islands, 61

spices, 61, 68

Swallow, 45

Swan, 33, 35, 45, 52

Sydenham, Elizabeth (second wife), 72, 87

T

Tavistock, England, 13, 14, 16

Ternate, Sultan of, 61

Terra Australis, 55

V

Virginia, 79

About the Author

Joy Paige is an editor, writer, and doll collector who lives in New York City. She credits her grandmother for her interest in books.

Photo Credits

Series Design
Tahara Hasan

Layout
Les Kanturek

Editor
Christine Poolos